MW00324855

A Story of the World Before the Fence

poems by

Leeya Mehta

Finishing Line Press
Georgetown, Kentucky

A Story of the World Before the Fence

ACKNOWLEDGMENTS

Grateful acknowledgement is made to the editors of the following publications,
in which versions of these poems originally appeared:

The Atlanta Review: "Refugees"
The Beloit Poetry Journal: "The Abduction"
Beltway Poetry Quarterly: "Metal Anniversary" & "The Years"
Chandrabhaga: "All of Me"
District Lit (& Reader's Choice Award Chapbook): "Black dog on the Anacostia
River"
Origins Journal (Issue: "Shame"): "Home /Tokyo"
Plume 6: "Women at the Peace Memorial / Hiroshima"
Plume Poetry: "Nudes I" & "Nudes II"
Poetry London: "The Towers of Silence"
Vinyl Poetry: "Fourth Street Plaza, National Gallery of Art, Washington DC" &
"Courthouse, Washington DC"
Gargoyle: CD #67 Recording: "Fourth Street Plaza"

Special thanks to Michael Anania, Ann Arbor, Vinod Balak, Diana Bolton, Joe
DiNunzio, Bina Sarkar Elias, Marlena Lynn, Nancy Kiang, Nancy Mitchell, Vivek
Narayanan, John Rosenwald, Rashmi Sadana, Tim Seibles, Dhun Sethna, Lee
Sharkey, Avi Shroff, Jessika Trancik, Ryan Tuggle, Santosh Verma and Randi Ward.
You are my angels.

Publisher: Leah Huete de Maines
Editor: Christen Kincaid
Cover Art: Vinod Balak, *Circumambulation*, 2019, http://www.galeriems.com/
Author Photo: Michaela Guerin Hackner
Cover Design: Elizabeth Maines McCleavy

Order online: www.finishinglinepress.com
also available on amazon.com

Author inquiries and mail orders:
Finishing Line Press
P. O. Box 1626
Georgetown, Kentucky 40324
U. S. A.

Table of Contents

REFUGEES
circa 917 AD

> "It will be well if we leave this country...and run away towards Ind for
> fear of life and religion's sake," said the head priest. Then a ship was made
> ready for the sea. Instantly they hoisted sail, placed the women and
> children in the vessel and rowed hard.
> —The Qissa-i Sanjan

The boat is too small for so many
and only the twin babies sleep,
drunk on milk and swaddled tight
rocking against their mother Armaiti
as the men row hard into the familiar waters
of the Gulf of Hormuz for the last time,
the starlight on the receding mountains
dimming fast until what is left
of this new moon night is the abiding
light from their holy fire, fed carefully
by their priest with sticks of sandalwood
pulled from deep in his white robes, as he looks east
into the black Arabian sea.

All the joy and blood that had come before
already turning to myth,
he counts how many generations
it takes to go from conqueror to refugee.

Gold bangles ring out as the twin babies are given
to their grandmother, then great grandmother,
and passed back to their mother, seventeen,
back erect, molten copper hair
fawn brown eyes flecked with green,
hiding tiger, quick to anger,
as quick to forgive the every day abuses girls
seem not to know they carry.

The father Sorab, twenty-five, son of Bezon,
named after his grandfather Sorab,
the same names alternating and
reaching back into the oldest Persian towns
winding up rivers into orchards,
where they planned this winter voyage,
had four boats in sight ahead,
and six behind him,
but now they are hidden by night
as they row with speed, the wind still,
the vessels arrows through the air.

So, when tired eyes stir with the new dawn
and the babies Bezon and Avan tug with little hands to drink,
steam from their breath against her chest,
their mother lifts her head as the men cry "Hindustan!"
she does not expect rose petal beach, like silk shivering before her.

Armaiti pulls herself to her knees to look
at this land at the waters edge that shifts and stirs
as if it is made of wings disturbed by the coming of her people
only to gasp, as flocks of long limbed flamingos
rise up into the sky and scatter,
revealing a sanctuary of white beach.

SLEEP

Island of Diu, coastal India, circa 917 AD

You know that feeling, when you are caught at the edge of sleep and consciousness,
too tired to stay awake even if the world is not safe enough to rest in—

Armaiti drifts into that place—
the clouds fine lines in the evening sky;

she is falling into new earth;
Bezon and Avan are milk-white rocks at either side, smoothed into oblivion.

She reaches for the voices that talk close by
but they do not remain long enough to comprehend,

before the words flap and are out of reach.
Their priest returns and his message makes her strain to wake, but she cannot.

She keeps dropping his words like heavy stones on the floor.
She does comprehend, though, that they may stay.

WELCOME

Gujarat, circa 936 AD

A priest said: "O Raja of Rajas, give us a place in this city: we are strangers seeking protection who have arrived in thy town."
—*The Qissa-i Sanjan*

They are told: her people may carry the past with them, every building, every word, even God, but they may not give it away to their new country.

They can remember, but they may not feed their old stories to their new neighbors as if they are the true God's food. They say, though there are many gods here, respect ours but do not give us yours.

They are told: keep your stories whole but separate.

They are told: keep your fire lit, cut wood for it in our forests, grow your own trees on our land, but do not take our children into your temples.

They are given jungle that stretches as far as the eye can see to a river. They plant their seeds from their old home, pomegranate, rose, sandalwood.

The local builders sit with them and plan homes. The sea is rich with rawas and mackerel. Dolphins call in the evening light. They teach the locals how to build better boats and plant orchards and flowers like their Persian gardens.

They flatter their new countrymen and add Krishna to their makeshift altars as they dig wells, and chop wood. The Portuguese arrive with Christ, they take him in. Worship the old gods, indulge the new.

Their fire burns quietly, it does not feast, it does not spread. They keep their promise.

For centuries, their numbers are small, then diminish. They have been too modest. Is it the price of real civilization?

THE TOWERS OF SILENCE

1

High on the hill,
beneath a fern sky of speckled spores
there is a place I long to describe
in a language I do not know.

The passing of each
beloved one into the rocks and
ivory heart of the pit
in that solitary place is not a passage
we will accept for ourselves, mother, you and I.
Nor did your father, who chose that box of fire,
only fire.

But the thought that we could all
rest together in the sepia shadow of a pit
drilled into the centre of the core —
that is not an empty wish, for after all,
where will our children go to find us?
Will they have to slice
through the shifting sky
like vultures,
searching for me and you and your father:
ashes choking the sea?

How we thought your father's
singed remains would be reduced
to one biscuit box, but saw instead
a suitcase of black static residue and
small pieces of bone and how you coughed —
wreaths of minute
grey dust rose through the chimney of Chandanvadi
into the soundless glare of that June day.

It is good, mother,
to have a resting place for family,
a spot to mourn the passing of the centuries
and that which we are;
to remember.

But there are places
that I long to describe
in a language I do not know.
And the Towers, by our not being in them,
that is our sacrifice.

2

If you are an outsider, not one of us, you would be interested to know what happens when we die. Most of my people, if we have been blessed by our exclusive priests in our special temples, in a language, Avesta, which is dead, if we haven't made the mistake of marrying a man who is one of you, will be carried up the hill in Mumbai on a cherished path, up two stairs or three, through a door and onto a cement bed at the edge of a precipice. The birds do their job (eating us), if there are enough of them, and our antibiotics do not make them sick; and our bones are swept into the pit. The men who provide this service are poor, lower caste and dedicated, they are born to this profession — body carriers, body sweepers, maintenance engineers of the Towers of Silence.

3

Must there be other words that can describe this place better than the ones I already know? Silent spectacles of words that form like clouds and beat thunderous drums with brocade batons.

4

Shadows in a garden of ochre thread;
vitiligo branches which echo
the brown whispers of a festering pea-hen;
hay fields, grass grown yellow from the start.

The English description of this hill is so still, so deathly quiet.

Some other language would make eloquent
this Hill that is soaked with human dead.
More distant than Hindi, Urdu, Gujarati, Marathi. These are
too close and yet impassive to my touch.

This is no English green, where graveyards rise, like fresh,
dew kissed soldiers in the valley of life.
No Tintern Abbey, roof collapsed,
not even a river here, blue and sweet.

This is one landscape
too burnt for English words,
there is no poetry
in the English sounds
nor richness in their beats.
Why look at this that escapes onto the page—
       there is a place high on a hill, surrounded by a
       malignancy of skyscrapers.
No rhythm there.
So there must be some other tongue to say—
this is a place I long to describe
in a language I do not know.

THE ABDUCTION
Lines composed in the Thar desert, six years after India's nuclear test

1

It's been six years since angels crossed the road at springtime.

Six years ago the Cherwell carried boats of scrolls whose black letters sliced through ivory sheets. We undid the blue ribbons and the words fell onto our feet, cutting our flesh. We bled. Our feet caked, shards of T's and Y's stuck out as we ran home in a sapphire meadow knee deep in water, grey spires suffocating as the wings came down in millions around us.

That night at the ball we crammed strawberries into angels' mouths but they would not keep silent. "The desert is so still at night," they said. "You can hear the shifting of the sand."

The juice from the berries dripped from their lips and splashed on our feet, burning them. "My stinging skin, where is my home, where is my home?" I asked. The night was fluorescent, your green dress fired cannonballs into the sky. "It is time to celebrate," you said, "not to mourn."

We danced. Fireflies in the desert broke into homes, hovered over sleeping children, entered bloodstreams, blew up spleens, burned up hearts, singed brains and livers.

"The desert rose to the sky," I said, but you had already forgiven them.

Your mouth covered my eyes, my tears made you spin round and round, your waist-length hair catching the strobe lights. Your seduction was complete, how could I resist you? You pleaded, "Love me. Love me," so I took your hand. "Dance," I said. I wished you were dead.

At seven o'clock no sun rose over the valley. The streets were empty as we dragged our trains home. You stopped for a moment to take up the fabric in your hands and then—as if you knew I would need something of you—you tore off the dirty train and stuffed it into my surprised hands.

Six years ago angels crossed the road at springtime in front of me. I stood in an emerald green dress, alone. They carried you away with them.

The empty street wound round the river's neck and as I crossed the bridge on the high street, I saw the boats sail out of view. I threw the green rag after them. I was free. I was free of you.

2

I have a memory of you alone in the night,
The rain outside, you screaming to belong,
My people you called them.
I will not accept that, I said, pushing you away,
These are not your people, these are not my people.
You wore your silver angel around your neck
As if it would protect you from hate.
Conquerors and conquered we have been
With such jewels of god hanging by our hearts.
Like the sand in the desert, you had believed
The burning train would never happen again,
That the women on their backs were the victims of barbarians,
Not our people.
"Why do you want to belong?" I had asked you.
Sometimes I feel belonging is like loving a corpse,
History's endless funerals.

3

I return without you to Bombay, the city of our birth. Memory is a curse; what have you done?

I search. I know that carved silver creature must be somewhere. You hadn't taken it with you the night of the ball, you had left it on the dresser by the window overlooking the crab apple tree. I must find that Asho Farohar, I must wear it, I must remember what happens when I hate, when I hate who we are because I fear our people are killers.

You could not understand why I do not like mirrors. In the mirror in the green dress we were the same person; my betrayal—when you decided silently in a room full of angels to leave me—was to let you go.

4

I have been looking for you in a hundred cities;
I have been calling your name;
I watch the mountains rise up in Tehran like
Vultures worshipping the sun;
I throw my net into the Arabian Sea and pull up
Skeletons of exiles who searched for land.

Hesitant in prayer, I stand in an ancestral fire temple in Udwada
Repeating softly, *humata, hukhta, huvarashta*
Good thoughts, good words, good deeds.
You are nowhere to be found.
Don't my children need to know who you are?

Finally, in Pokhran, in an ancient *haveli* with
A Hindu shrine that leads off from a courtyard full of peacocks
I sit silently watching for a sign.
Shadows of women dressed in mirror work skirts
Skip up stairs in a house opposite me.
The sand moans, the well runs dry, when will you return?
Don't my children need to know who we are?

5

It's been six years since angels crossed the road at springtime.
They have returned this time without sending word.
I wake up to drink water, leaning out of the window
Overlooking Bombay harbor
Where ships pause, guns pointed to the sky.

I hear the shredding of cloth.
From the black-green islands in the sea they rise,
Their transparent bodies the color of night;
The moon shining through their ferocious faces.

I run, I am out on the street before they are.
They drop to the ground and stand still staring at me with their liquid eyes.
Then they cross the road and walk slowly away.
Except for one.
You.

They have brought you back and though
I want to celebrate your return,
You complete me with your exile.
I know I cannot take you back.

DECORUM

Women at the Peace Memorial, Hiroshima

> *"The heart never fits the journey"*
> —*Island and Figs, Jack Gilbert*

This was not about you
This was not about me
We were
the picture book couple
Only to them.

White men had dropped bombs on their faces
Yet they wanted to embrace us, bless us,
Make sure they would be the last ones to
Need a new vocabulary for extermination.
Pikadon.
Pika = atomic bomb light.
Don = the sound of the bomb.

The first woman saw you
So handsome, with your long blond hair
Hiding your irreverent blue eyes.
She asked if you were American
And you said, no, English,
Which eased the tension just a little bit.

She saw me
In love with you
And assumed
We could all abandon our restraint
And pray for peace.
So you and I stood in a manicured park under phoenix trees
And held hands for the first time.

I have a confession to make
I have never been taught how to pray,
Especially in public.
It frightened me to touch this
Strange woman, her long face reorganized
By burns carried for half a century
Her forehead where her eyes should be;

Suppose she could enter my mind,
Leaving shards of memories
That would cut me?

But you squeezed my hand tight
Even after we had moved away
And whispered to me that
My mind had the power to keep itself safe
From wandering spirits. You had walked
The Camino de Santiago,
So you knew: it was all up to me.
You are a pilgrim, always in search of god.
They could leave you out in a desert
Without your shoes and you would labor
A hundred days if you had a church at the end of the road.

I had walked with you for hours
Through floors of death
But after this peace museum I knew
I had never been tested.
I do not know what I would do in a desert;
You cannot assume anything of yourself
Until you have experienced fire.

This woman, Setsuko, was six years old in 1945,
She was on her way to school, balancing on the back
Of a silver bicycle with a red bell
That her mother was riding when
The Enola Gay flew over Mount Hiji.

Hours later, on our way to dinner,
The other woman stopped us unexpectedly
In the middle of a crosswalk
She was as tiny as a sparrow with
A round dough face,
"You are so happy," she said,
"You are married, I bless you."
Then she hugged us both,
And I felt in her all the love which she had saved
For her mother, her father, her husband,

And her baby,
All dead in one day.

What is this place where you can resurrect yourself
After you have been completely ruined?

Neither woman knew
How much we needed them,
So we could pretend,
For just a moment,
That we were this glorious thing.
The world had changed.
I was given so many signs that words like
Decorum did not fit it anymore.
That I was meant to kiss you first.

The women were blind to
How unrequited my love was;
Yet how big they conceived it to be.
No one should keep such love
Unspoken, for it will drive you mad;
Only by giving it away will you be safe again.

HOME

Tokyo

The river comes to view in the darkness
A light across the bank is burning softly
The homeless are asleep, except this man
Who warms his face, as he drinks himself to life.
It is two a.m., the birds as big as dogs are restless
In their nests in the cherry blossom trees.

The fire across the bank goes out; the sun's white light
Illuminates a highway with bands of speeding trucks;
Six a.m. again and I am here in a place
Where a restless morning sun is a measure of my heart.
I walk past an empty swimming pool and tennis courts,
Temples and school yards, neighborhoods with kumquat trees in front yards
Still I cannot shake you, a fellow traveler in a strange land,
To whom I will never confess my love.

I tremble through each breakfast
My stomach ready for a race;
I lose my possessions on trains,
On buses, in the rain my slippers lie forgotten;
The gravel on the road is too real under my feet;
The swooping of typhoons skins my scalp.

I can keep walking through the night
If you are here beside me, as you often are;
The quiet light across the bank carries a silent meaning
When you brush against my hand—
It is the struggle of those who fall outside
Of love and can't return.

So far from our homes and from our measured safety
I choose a perfect moment I know I can sustain,
Not just blind love, but the permanence of love—
Love outside of you —for we will never be husband and wife
And I will never be the woman on her bicycle
Bringing home fresh fish to cook for you and our child;
Nor will we pop a bottle in the rain, like this homeless man,
Speaking only to strangers, never to the ones we love.

I watch the way your face changes
With the day, the lines steadily spreading below your eyes
Because I make you laugh.
I watch my face in the mirror in my hotel room as the steam
Rises up from a tub the size of a baby's cot;
In a few days of knowing you, my laughter has returned.

What is love, I want to ask. Is it steadfastness or
Is it the crazy certainty of gently carrying a
Steady state of nervousness?
It is lying beside you in the darkness never making love;
It is crossing from my dreams into yours and dragging you back
From night terrors that haunt you even when you are so far
From those who are buried because justice was too late.

At first I think you are less afraid of home than I am, but now I know
It is the softness of England that makes you hate it, makes you seek out wars.

When I leave you on a cold summer's morning, clouds gather fast;
The final typhoon grabs my hair
Pulling me forward into my next life;
Left behind, you stand, amazed at the stars in the sky,
A million cells I gifted you to celebrate that walk
On hard cement beside a river
Where men never go home because they're ashamed of who they are.

BLACK DOG ON THE ANACOSTIA RIVER

Suddenly alone, I run down the hill
Through Japanese gardens

In search of signs
That will tell me I am home in this new life

In this American city ten thousand miles
Away from my own choking Arabian Sea.

The Anacostia River appears,
A brown knot of sludge

A dragon aching, its old feathers
Listless in the afternoon sun

No forty-foot glittering wingspan rising up to
Ripe cornfields, towering sunflowers

This is how I find it this September day
A flooded marshland resting.

Then a flash of black,
Shining, molten, fast moving

Rottweiler, circling, its jaws set square,
Its eyes on me, all menace

I think, the heart of an animal is unseen
It could go for the jugular

But the dog flashes out of sight along chain fence—
Maybe it knows I am with child

Though I do not—
As if it wants distance too

As if it is the heart of man that is unknown
And I am the omen of how we abandon the things we should love.

THE YEARS

1

Sometimes I feel like
I came to the New World for the snow,
to wear my great grandmother's Japanese coat
brittle from under use in a flat in Bombay.

My first winter in Washington, we were crossing Wisconsin Avenue
across from the gas station at the corner of Calvert Street,
it was November and you were freezing
and coming down with a cold.
(You, who had grown up in the American West
where snow chains on tires delivered you to school.)
It was becoming very dark
and I was warm.
What right did I have to be so warm, I asked myself?

2

In the middle of another winter,
I sat under your oil painting—
sky the color of robin's eggs
ochre hay, pistachio grass.

3

"This is my home," I showed you in Bombay,
and we were happy there that month
with the bad turkey and the dear friends.

For years I would not return—
all I need is here, as wife, as mother.

But you know,
the longing for what you cannot have
will keep you from settling anywhere.

4

Our first child is the sun
you orbit.

You have a warm coat now, you are not sad
through the long, wet winters.

You are trying to understand
the inevitable—
you have grown up.

5

The journey away from me to you
has left me lost.
I know I cannot go on this way.

6

Through the coast of Maine
hand in hand with our little girl,
I lessen my hold on you
yet affirm that I carry you inside me.
You are a good father.

7

I am weak, grief makes me weak—
you do not love me.
Your strength is an affront.
It is inevitable.
We are practicing loss.

8

Then another child, fat as a caterpillar,
conceived in that bed in Maine with a bad mattress,
replenishes us.
You make me laugh again,
We are not what we were.

We lose our possessions in a fire.
People tell us when we begin to miss them
we will be back to normal.
I miss nothing.

9

The origin of love is like the origin of music;
one cannot know the music of the heart
until one has loved;
one cannot know what the body needs
without listening to the body.
You have listened well, my body knows you.

10

The ground in the winter
starts out hard.
Then the snow comes and it is hidden
under white layers that get heavier and heavier
turning to thin sheets of glass that crack and pack
and cut the earth.
The glass disintegrates in rainstorms;
mist obscures light from the forest floor;
the ground is clogged with water, it gives way underfoot;
magnificent stags, with brown antlers rising up in the fog,
guard the undergrowth, as if it is full of diamond fern.

We are not from this patch of earth,
we came from another part of it, but we will return to
swamp, this forest floor that brings forth your beautiful peonies
and the steam of summer.

11

The dance is on
but the music's new;
beware the ice and
find reasons to move to keep warm.
Stay indoors sometimes and regard what you have with joy,
hold it close when it is here before you
for it may not return
with the certainty that brings
winter back.

NUDES I

Bathhouse, Hakone, Japan

Once I cross the threshold
I take off my clothes.
Mirrors in the room register my body
but for now they are superfluous;
later, when I re-enter the familiar world,
I may care how I look, my face
perfectly poised at the moment of reflection.

I follow the other women to the line of showers,
sit on a plastic stool,
slowly wash my hair with liquid soap.
My body scrubbed
I soak in the bone hot bath,
as steam from the springs unseals my pores,
peach flowers in bloom.
Beyond the windows, mountains and still lake
protect a red core of magma, resting, scalding.

All are naked here, I am
a recognizable female form
of no differentiated quality.

NUDES II

Bathhouse, Centreville, Virginia

My friends are getting older; laughter sits deep in their bodies,
and spills out of their eyes like the morning sun.
We do not notice if we are physically alike
or unlike each other even though we are naked today,
hidden only occasionally by water.
We do not look for comparison,
do not measure smallness or girth.
Between steam and ice and clay and stone
who is watching? No one.

NUDES III

Fourth Street Plaza, National Gallery of Art, Washington DC

Our child kicks off her sandals,
breathing in the wild summer.
Hot cobblestones beneath her smarting feet,
she races into the empty plaza
toward fountain and glass, throwing off cotton dress.
In her underwear, water flecks her four-year old belly.
Body merging with the pale pink marble façade,
she laughs the world away.
Eyes ripped with fury, the guard rages,
"Put on her clothes or I'll call Family Services.
He points east, "It is there, just there."
We slip the dress back on our glistening child,
a fawn confused by this water hole,
curious that these teeth of glass are skylights
lighting a concourse beneath her feet.
She walks
on the roof of civilization.

NUDES IV

Courthouse, Washington DC

Before words
there is body.
The break out scream of life—a child born—
the body demands food, seeks comfort, likes to be clean.
Before words, there is laughter.

East of the Roman city, a man is standing trial
for repeatedly putting his naked baby
under scalding water to clean him.
Skin separates from skin with second-degree burns;
the fluid filled blisters changing the surface of this city.
His frustration runs like the coils of the freeway that
divides this city—East and West.
The man breathes, a filament of space—
a moment's refuge from the courthouse, the closing in of cops, lawyer, judge—
his mind travels to the last sight of home
as he was taken away at dusk:
the locked, rusted gate that leads to wide span of riverbank,
and there, just out of reach, but visible,
abandoned grass at the water's edge;
white flames of egrets nesting in a tree on the other bank;
a commuter train flees past; and headlights from the freeway come on
while the power plant that once moaned and clattered
looms silent in the twilight, waiting to be torn down.
The old life over, the east cleared and preened anew.
Someone in the courtroom is talking about childhood:
the sound of children playing outdoors, of evening safety,
of milk and kindness before sleep, that babies laugh the most at bed time.

When has this man's body ever been sacred?
It remembers everything but laughter—
swallows disappearing into the evening sky.

METAL ANNIVERSARY

A quiet steel river winds its way from our place in the trees
To that Old Town where we slipped bands of gold
On each other's fingers
Hand-made in a factory in Bombay
Where once I walked every day on a
Mottled tar road near a rusted sea.
Heavy, like iron, you expect the years to sit
But they are light, like dreams of blue copper domes.
Not cold, like steel, on this winter's day
But warm, like your mouth, and this well heated apartment.
Nor hard, like titanium, aloof and unchangeable
But soft, like cesium butter, spread on fresh baked bread.
We can be lighter, warmer, softer,
Kinder; this day reminds me of that.

TIN

Marriage seems a challenge thrown out
to a flimsy flock—
what do you know of anything
ten years in, and you haven't even fought
a war?

We admit, there is much to do.
Hours packed like sardines into that
morning madness of barely an hour
and then the labor of the day
which runs afoul by night.
Appearing at seven p.m.,
yes, post noon,
is a tin cry
as she is easily bent out of shape
and he is 'a dull-gray powdery material with no common uses other than a
few specialized semiconductor applications. These two allotropes, α-tin and
β-tin, are more commonly known as gray tin and white tin, respectively.'

Blah blah blah.
Enough of the flotsam, the jetsam, the
wild reckless self-pitying Mariner.
Marriage is a fine life. *Yo dada!* our children cry.

Thus, facts that should be celebrated:
1. We are soft and malleable.
2. We do not corrode in water.
3. 'In cold conditions, β-tin tends to transform
    spontaneously into α-tin, a phenomenon known
    as "tin pest."'
4. Tin is the 49th most abundant element in Earth's crust.
5. Love is the most abundant element in our house.
    And yes, clutter competes.

FENCES

In Memorium, ALB, 1975-2016

I

It wasn't just me, we were all waiting for you
to walk into the room,
your eyes unspooling with ideas
for your four small children;
big earrings drawing away attention
from your hair, tied in a peach scarf I gave you,
the softest one I owned,
worn all through my happy college days,
before we knew one another,
you, a girl from Washington who loved life,
me, a girl from Bombay who saw your genius for living.

At the end, my friend, you walked slowly, but you were
determined not to stop, holding on to our grateful arms,
each step your secret pact with yourself
to keep us all weaving your children's lives into our own.

In less than six months,
you were gone —Easter day, you were forty.
That scarf disappeared, unlike you,
into some forgotten place.

You liked your tea like I did,
Irish breakfast, milk and sugar.
Alone, at home, I imagine making an extra cup
to pass to you as you lie on the couch,
your dog nearby,
your back broken,
planning a trip around the block with our children
to plant milkweed bushes for monarch butterflies
in the elementary school gardens.

After it happened,
I would walk in the woods and see
dogs wandering into the underbrush and disappearing.
They'd return smiling and unscrewed,
for they'd had an adventure:
somewhere inside the torn mess of twigs
you had taken their heads in your hands and tickled their ears;
a warning that the screws of love sit deep in the bone.

II

Perhaps you wander through the forest;
your long dark hair and red hood startling runners.

There are tales of coyotes in the night
digging up mustard gas canisters.
In the northwest parcels of Washington,
mansions conceal laboratories.
Poisoned gardens burst with heads of cabbage
left uneaten. Bottled water sits piled on kitchen tables.
The hundred-year-old military-industrial state.
The local cost of fighting wars elsewhere.

As I trudge through the trees in the overexposed noon, perhaps
I see monarch butterflies weaving a living crown for you,
as your children's voices rise out of the playground,
close enough to hear, but not to see.

III

They tell a story of the world
before the fence.

A brown herd of deer, led by their King
came out of the clay forest splintering the leafless filigree.
Hooves padded out of undergrowth, up the steep driveway
into my pristine garden with glass breezeways
lined with decorated Christmas trees.

Even in the numbing cold, the deer smelled roses
as bushes lay dormant, stamens burned.

A carousel, they wove around the circular courtyard with joy,
the night sky filled with the blessing of
snow falling softly on warm snouts
until the King broke away and
bounded into the unseen glass, antlers raised,
shattering it.

You lived in Chevy Chase Washington then,
but like so many things, I'll never have a chance
to ask if you heard
this happened in my apartment building
on your twenty-fifth birthday, a Christmas night.

Rolls of wire arrived by Easter;
the beheaded stag—a case for fences.

I lived in Bombay then, and came to this city
a few years after the fence.

Now deer collect in insecure clusters,
snouts like cherry buds in the mist,
hind legs twitching, whites of eyes flashing,
uncertain of how barriers can keep
wandering spirits separate from those they love.

ALL OF ME

When I am old
and I am blind
will you carry me,
your fingers bending backwards with the weight of me?

When I am dying
take me down to that place
we were never sure love would last
like the sound that day, of the sea.

When I am old
and I am blind
and you are not allowed to rest but I can
for my heart beat slows from being carried so long,
you will know all of me—
and it will make your pulse race

for you are the love who never minded
the weight of me.

MOTHER'S DAY

I have traveled ten thousand miles with you,
From a small apartment at the edge of the water in a city piled high into the
sky—
Stacks of cement boxes with bathrooms and bedrooms
Furniture, people, parrots, dogs, washing machines
And the rare laburnum tree with bunches of gold flowers
That breaks the steady state of squalor that marks these
Still beautiful Bombay streets—
To rural Virginia where in the spring, lace white pear trees
Make the world seem perfect, no underlying hint of violence
Or suffering to mark what is coming for each of us.

When you think of me,
Irritable, home sick, carrying my burdens badly,
Burying my laughter deep,
Don't forget that I see
A red cardinal shooting across a brown garden,
A piece of blue sky,
An orange sunset over a wide river.

When I think of you,
Lonely, too attentive to daytime TV
That keeps you connected to the outside world,
Don't forget that I see
The laughter of generations in your heart
In languages so old all human secrets are safe with them
Turning yellow and stale with under use.

There are many things that make a life,
One of them is love, the acceptance I have of you.
But what of laughter, mother, will it not help
When it is the end and there is nothing to mask what is coming for us?
What will abide if my children do not know Gujarati
And cannot laugh with us at our old family jokes?
But then I look around the room and see my children laugh a lot anyway,
Like wild flowers they find a crack in the concrete to burst out and reveal that
The time has come to forgive myself for what we have lost
And learn to live again in a new country with pear trees.

Leeya Mehta is a prize-winning poet, fiction writer and essayist. She is the author of *The Towers of Silence* and writes a popular column on the reading & writing life, *The Company We Keep*.

Poems in *A Story of the World Before the Fence* have received an International Publication Award from the *Atlanta Review*; a Readers' Choice Award from District Lit; twice nominated for a Pushcart Prize; and a Finalist in the 18th Annual Arts and Letters Rumi Prize for Poetry. A version of the chapbook was a Semi-Finalist for the Black River Chapbook Competition, *Black Lawrence Press*; and received honorable mention from the Women of Resilience Chapbook Contest, *Southern Collective*.

Leeya was born into a Parsi Zoroastrian family in Bombay. The Zoroastrian Parsis of India trace their descent in different waves from Persia over the last thousand years. They first sought refuge in the tenth century A.D. in Udwada, and other sites on the western coast of India. There are about a hundred thousand Parsis remaining in the world. Nurtured by her mother Avi's theatre community, Leeya performed on stage and did radio through school and at St Xavier's College, where poet Eunice de Souza mentored her. She spent much of her childhood living with her mother and maternal grandparents, Armaity and Sorab, whose apartment overlooked the Arabian Sea. Armaity wrote poetry and loved nature. Leeya's poetry explores the intimate space of the family and how it relates to the physical geography of cities and nature.

Leeya spent two years at Oxford University receiving a Master of Arts in Philosophy, Politics, and Economics (PPE) on a Radhakrishnan British Chevening Scholarship. When her mother moved to America, Leeya followed. She received a Master's in Public Policy from Georgetown University and works at the World Bank. After travels in the Arctic borderlands and a fellowship in Human Rights in Japan, she lives in Washington DC, volunteering for numerous literary organizations as an editor, contest judge and on the board of the Inner Loop Lit. She has recently completed a novel, *Extinction*. Find her work at www.leeyamehta.com

PRAISE FOR *A Story of The World Before The Fence*

This remarkable collection begins with a series of poems that vividly recount a migration by boat, presumably carrying Mehta's distant ancestors, from 10th century Iran to the west coast of India, the dazzle of arrival in a wildly fertile land and the enduring experience of being separate… Displacements, ancestral and personal, inform the whole of this collection. Poems set in India, Japan and Washington, DC richly describe scenes of personal and domestic life in a world, its ancient, informing faith would remind us, that is defined everywhere by individual, moral choice. The fence of the book's title is a literal fence in Washington, erected to keep a herd of deer in place, but it is, as well, another figure of separation and mortality. At the close of the book's final poem Mehta says, "It is time for me to forgive myself for what we have lost," a consolation, certainly but yet another accepted responsibility.

—**Michael Anania**

Through centuries and across continents, Leeya Mehta evokes the transgenerational trauma of her ancestors, the Zoroastrian Parsis, to narratively structure an intimate, feminocentric experience of cultural and personal displacement. Her haunting poems, with their hard-won wisdom and exquisite imagery, serve as "a warning that the screws of love sit deep in the bone" despite—yet, perhaps, because of—the various forms of exile that complicate identities, relationships, and senses of place. *A Story of the World Before the Fence* acknowledges "how barriers can keep / wandering spirits separate from those they love," but it nevertheless consoles us with the miracle that is laughter: a universal language that can still anchor us to one another and help us learn to forgive ourselves for what we have lost along the way.

—**Randi Ward**

Whether tracing the 10th century journey of religious refugees from Persia to a tender but continually ambivalent asylum in India or dwelling in the complicities and solidarities of our own era, this is a troubled look at belonging, where belonging is ever "like loving a corpse" among "history's endless funerals". Mehta's compassion and clear, unhurried tone leaven the seriousness and ambition of the work's intellectual horizons, and an emotional power and turbulence as deep as that in certain moods of its Anacostia River: "brown knot of sludge, // a dragon aching."

—**Vivek Narayanan**

CPSIA information can be obtained
at www.ICGtesting.com
Printed in the USA
BVHW070911221120
593557BV00002B/84